The Quest

-FOR KIDS-

AN EXPEDITION TOWARD A DEEPER RELATIONSHIP WITH GOD

YOUNGER KIDS ACTIVITY BOOK
BETH MOORE
WITH KATHY STRAWN
LIFEWAY PRESS®
NASHVILLE, TN

Requests for permission should be addressed in writing to
LifeWay Press®
One LifeWay Plaza
Nashville, TN 37234-0172

ISBN 9781535909594
Item 005804821

Dewey Decimal Classification Number: 268.432
Subject Heading: Discipleship—Curricula\God\Bible—Study
Dewey Decimal Classification Number: 248.82
Subject Heading: CHRISTIAN LIFE \ JESUS CHRIST—TEACHINGS

Printed in the United States of America
LifeWay Kids
LifeWay Resources
One LifeWay Plaza
Nashville, Tennessee 37234-0172

We believe the Bible has God for its author; salvation for its end; and truth, without any mixture of error, for its matter and that all Scripture is totally true and trustworthy. To review LifeWay's doctrinal guideline, please visit *lifeway.com/doctrinalguideline*.

All Scripture quotations are taken from the Christian Standard Bible

® Copyright 2017 by Holman Bible Publishers. Used by permission.

Table of Contents

MATTHEW 7:7-11. 4

MEETING ONE
THE QUEST: GROWING CLOSER TO GOD IS OUR QUEST 6

MEETING TWO
THE QUEST AND FAITH: FOLLOWING GOD'S PLAN 12

MEETING THREE
THE QUEST AND FEAR: TRUSTING AND DEPENDING ON GOD . . . 18

MEETING FOUR
THE QUEST AND DIFFICULT TIMES: CLINGING CLOSE TO GOD 24

MEETING FIVE
THE QUEST AND OTHERS: GROWING CLOSER TO GOD THROUGH SERVICE . 30

MEETING SIX
THE QUEST AND PROMISE: GOD WILL GO WITH US TO THE END. 36

PARENT GUIDE 42

CERTIFICATE. 48

MATTHEW 7:7-11

8 FOR EVERYONE WHO ASKS RECEIVES, AND THE ONE WHO SEEKS FINDS AND TO THE ONE WHO KNOCKS, THE DOOR WILL BE OPENED.

7 ASK, AND IT WILL BE GIVEN TO YOU. SEEK AND YOU WILL FIND. KNOCK AND THE DOOR WILL BE OPENED TO YOU.

⁹ WHO AMONG YOU, IF HIS SON ASKS HIM FOR **BREAD**, WILL GIVE HIM A A STONE?

¹⁰ OR IF HE **ASKS** FOR A **FISH**, WILL GIVE HIM A **SNAKE?**

¹¹ IF YOU THEN, WHO ARE EVIL, KNOW HOW TO GIVE **GOOD GIFTS** TO YOUR CHILDREN, **HOW MUCH MORE** WILL YOUR FATHER IN HEAVEN GIVE GOOD THINGS **TO THOSE WHO ASK HIM.**

The Quest

GROWING CLOSER TO GOD
IS OUR QUEST

Quest —

an act of seeking;

a search in order to find or get something

THROUGHOUT THIS STUDY, TOGETHER WE WILL BE ON A QUEST TO GROW CLOSER TO GOD. THE BIBLE TELLS US GOD HAS ALSO BEEN ON A QUEST TO SAVE US AND BRING US CLOSER TO HIM.

GOD'S VERY GOOD PLAN

In the beginning, nothing existed except God. God went to work. He spoke and created light. He separated the water on earth from the water above the earth to make the sky. God made the dry land and the seas. He commanded the earth to grow plants and trees. He placed the sun, moon, and stars in the sky.

God created all living things in the water and all birds that fly. He added animals to cover the earth. God looked down at His creation and knew that it was good.

God created people. He made people special. God created people in His own image. God made a man, Adam, from dust of the ground. He breathed into the man, and the man became alive. God took a rib from the man and created a woman. Adam named his wife Eve.

God instructed the man and woman to care for the garden where He had placed them and to take care of the earth. God warned Adam and Eve: "You may eat of any tree in the garden except that you must not eat of the tree of knowledge of good and evil. If you eat of this tree, you will die."

The serpent questioned Eve. "Did God really say that you cannot eat of any tree in the garden?" he asked. Eve answered, "We can eat of any tree except the one in the middle of the garden. God told us we would die if we eat it or touch it." Satan lied, "No! You won't die. God just knows that if you eat the fruit, you will be like Him, knowing good and evil."

The fruit of the tree looked so good. Eve thought about being as wise as God. She took some of the fruit and ate it. She gave some to Adam to eat. He knew it was wrong to eat the fruit,, but he ate it anyway.

Suddenly Adam and Eve realized they had no clothes on. They sewed leaves together to cover themselves. That evening, Adam and Eve heard God walking in the garden. They quickly hid themselves. God called to Adam, "Where are you?"

Adam answered, I heard you in the garden. I was afraid since I have no clothes on. So I hid." God asked, "Who told you that you were naked? Did you eat of the tree I told you not to eat from?" Adam blamed Eve and God. "The woman You made for me gave me fruit and I ate it." When God asked what she had done, Eve blamed the serpent. "The serpent tricked me," she said.

God punished the serpent. He punished Eve. He punished Adam. Yet, God also gave Adam and Eve hope. He promised that one day a descendant of Adam and Eve would crush the serpent. God clothed Adam and Eve in animal skins. God sent them from the garden.

—based on Genesis 1–3

A-MAZE-ING FACTS

Draw a line through the maze to discover the answer to each question. Can you find all six paths? Hint: It helps to use a different color for each path!

ADAM

2 HOW WAS EVE TRICKED?

6 WHO DID ADAM BLAME FOR HIS SIN?

THE SERPENT LIED TO HER.

EVE

4 WHAT DID ADAM AND EVE DO WHEN GOD CAME THROUGH THE GARDEN?

3 TO WHOM DID EVE GIVE FRUIT?

HID

WHERE ARE YOU?

5 WHAT DID GOD ASK ADAM AS HE CAME THROUGH THE GARDEN?

1 WHO TRICKED EVE INTO EATING THE FRUIT?

THE SERPENT

BACKPACK TALK

Pack up for the quest! Fill in the blanks on the backpack using the words from the objects around it. Find out some things you can do to grow closer to God.

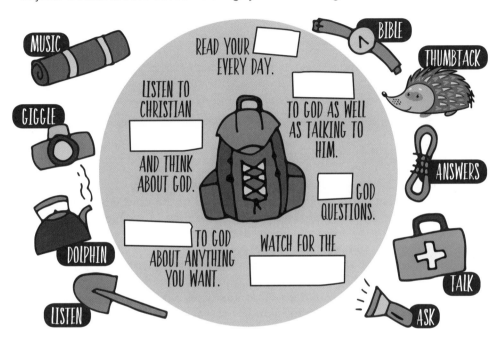

MUSIC

GIGGLE

DOLPHIN

LISTEN

READ YOUR ☐ EVERY DAY.

LISTEN TO CHRISTIAN ☐ AND THINK ABOUT GOD.

☐ TO GOD ABOUT ANYTHING YOU WANT.

BIBLE

THUMBTACK

ANSWERS

☐ TO GOD AS WELL AS TALKING TO HIM.

☐ GOD QUESTIONS.

WATCH FOR THE ☐

TALK

ASK

☑ Print your initials above the way you like best to get closer to God.
☑ Draw a star on one you will try to do this week.
☑ Put a check mark beside one you will try to do some place besides home.

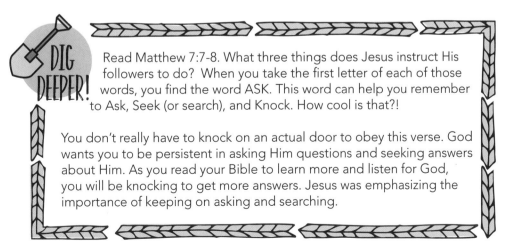

DIG DEEPER!

Read Matthew 7:7-8. What three things does Jesus instruct His followers to do? When you take the first letter of each of those words, you find the word ASK. This word can help you remember to Ask, Seek (or search), and Knock. How cool is that?!

You don't really have to knock on an actual door to obey this verse. God wants you to be persistent in asking Him questions and seeking answers about Him. As you read your Bible to learn more and listen for God, you will be knocking to get more answers. Jesus was emphasizing the importance of keeping on asking and searching.

MY DAILY QUERIES

Queries? You may be asking, "What in the world are queries?" Then you would be querying! Queries are just another name for questions. At the end of each week's study, you will have two pages to use privately as you talk to God, ask Him questions, and seek to grow closer to Him.

Each day will have a Bible passage for you to read and think about. It may have questions to spark your thinking or explanations about the verses. Each day will have space for you to journal your thoughts, feelings, and questions to God. If you miss a day, just start where you left off the last time.
Okay. Ready, set, query!

DAILY QUERY 1

Read Genesis 3:8-11 and underline the questions God asks:
Then the man and his wife heard the sound of the Lord God walking in the garden at the time of the evening breeze, and they hid from the Lord God among the trees of the garden. So the Lord God called out to the man and said to him, "Where are you?"

And he said, "I heard you in the garden, and I was afraid because I was naked, so I hid."

Then he asked, "Who told you that you were naked? Did you eat from the tree that I commanded you not to eat from?"

One of the reasons God asks questions even though He knows the answers is that He wants people to grow closer to Him.

➤ What are some questions you wish God would answer?

➤ Write down your questions or things you want to pray to God about.

DAILY QUERY 2

Read Genesis 1:26-27: Then God said, "Let us make man in our image, according to our likeness. They will rule the fish of the sea, the birds of the sky, the livestock, the whole earth, and the creatures that crawl on the earth." So God created man in his own image; he created him in the image of God; he created them male and female.
➤ Circle in this passage everything the Bible says about the people God created.

➤ God loves you! Make a list of your favorite things about yourself. Pray, thanking God for all the ways He has blessed you.

DAILY QUERY 3

Read Genesis 3:2-6: The woman said to the serpent, "We may eat the fruit from the trees in the garden. But about the fruit of the tree in the middle of the garden, God said, 'You must not eat it or touch it, or you will die.'" "No! You will not die," the serpent said to the woman. "In fact, God knows that when you eat it your eyes will be opened and you will be like God, knowing good and evil." The woman saw that the tree was good for food and delightful to look at, and that it was desirable for obtaining wisdom. So she took some of its fruit and ate it; she also gave some to her husband, who was with her, and he ate it.

➤ Circle the words that tell what Eve's choice was in this passage. What did she choose?

➤ Eve disobeyed God and did what she wanted. Is there a time when you have done the same? Write about that here.

➤ Ask God for forgiveness. He loves you and will forgive you.

DAILY QUERY 4

Read Genesis 3:8-10: Then the man and his wife heard the sound of the Lord God walking in the garden at the time of the evening breeze, and they hid from the Lord God among the trees of the garden. So the Lord God called out to the man and said to him, "Where are you?" And he said, "I heard you in the garden, and I was afraid because I was naked, so I hid."

➤ Circle the word that tells what Adam was feeling in the garden as he hid from God.

➤ Why was Adam afraid?

➤ There are different kinds of being afraid. Adam was afraid because he knew he had disobeyed God.

➤ When have you been most afraid? What might have helped you be less afraid?

Journal how you feel during times you are afraid. Tell God how these verses reassure you or what other kinds of help you want from Him. Ask for His guidance during frightening times.

DAILY QUERY 5

Read Psalm 139:14 and 16: I will praise you because I have been remarkably and wondrously made. Your works are wondrous, and I know this very well. Your eyes saw me when I was formless; all my days were written in your book and planned before a single one of them began.

➤ Think about how you are wonderfully made. Think about "how much more" God loves you than anyone else loves you.

➤ List several things you like about yourself.

The Quest & Faith

FOLLOWING GOD'S PLAN

Search —

to look into or over carefully or thoroughly

in an effort to find or discover something.

GOD WANTS US TO SEARCH THE SCRIPTURES CAREFULLY
TO LEARN MORE ABOUT GOD AND HIS PLAN FOR US.

ABRAM'S JOURNEY

Abram lived with his wife, Sarai. One day, God called out to Abram. God had chosen Abram and told him to leave home and move to a place where he had never been. God promised Abram three things: a large family, land for his family, and blessing. Later, God visited Abram in a vision and said, "Do not be afraid, Abram. I am your shield; your reward will be very great."

God's promise was good, but Abram was sad because he didn't have any children to inherit his blessing. "One of my slaves will be my heir," Abram cried. But God's plan was boundless. He let Abram outside to remind him of His promise. "Look at the sky and count the stars, if you can," God said. Abram couldn't count the stars. There were too many! "Your family will be that numerous," God promised. Abram believed God, and God was pleased.

God also promised that Abram's family would keep the land they were living in. Abram asked, "How can I be sure?" So God confirmed His covenant with Abram.

God told Abram to bring five animals: a cow, a goat, a ram, a turtledove, and a pigeon. Abram did as God said, and he divided the animals. Then, when the sun was setting, a deep sleep came over him.

While Abram slept, God told him what would happen in the future. He said that Abram's family would be slaves in another country for 400 years. After these 400 years, God would judge the nation and bless Abram's family. And God promised that in spite of all the difficult things would happen, Abram would live a long and peaceful life.

After sunset, once it was dark, a smoking pot of fire and a flaming torch representing God passed between the divided animals. This sign demonstrated that God would be responsible for keeping His promise.

—based on Genesis 12:1-3 and Genesis 15:1-21

FALLING BLOCKS

Figure out where each set of letter blocks should fall in the empty grid. Write the letters in their proper places.

Now read the sentence you made! Do you agree?

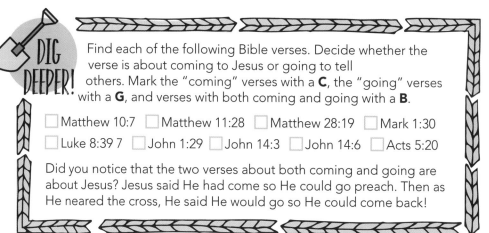

DIG DEEPER!

Find each of the following Bible verses. Decide whether the verse is about coming to Jesus or going to tell others. Mark the "coming" verses with a **C**, the "going" verses with a **G**, and verses with both coming and going with a **B**.

- ☐ Matthew 10:7
- ☐ Matthew 11:28
- ☐ Matthew 28:19
- ☐ Mark 1:30
- ☐ Luke 8:39 7
- ☐ John 1:29
- ☐ John 14:3
- ☐ John 14:6
- ☐ Acts 5:20

Did you notice that the two verses about both coming and going are about Jesus? Jesus said He had come so He could go preach. Then as He neared the cross, He said He would go so He could come back!

ABRAM DOT-TO-DOT

Read each statement from the Bible story. Draw a line from statement to statement in the order it happened.

Abram took his wife Sarai and his nephew Lot and moved as God directed.

God promised Abram and Sarai that she have a baby before a year was over.

Abram pleaded with God to save the city if at least 10 right-living people could be found.

God told Abram to leave his land and go to a place God would show him.

Isaac, whose name means laughter, was born to Sarai and Abram when he was 100 years old and she was 90.

God made a covenant with Abram in which He promised to give Abram land and more children than grains of sand on the shore.

IF YOU LOOK AT THE DESIGN YOU MADE, YOU WILL SEE PART OF GOD'S PROMISE TO ABRAHAM:
YOUR DESCENDANTS WILL BE AS NUMEROUS AS THE ―――――――――――
IN THE ――――――――――――. GENESIS 22:17

MY DAILY QUERIES

Each day will have a Bible passage for you to read and think about. It may have questions to spark your thinking or explanations about the verses. Each day will have space for you to journal your thoughts, feelings, and questions to God. It's true that God knows our thoughts whether we write them or not, but sometimes writing them helps us get things more firmly fixed in our hearts and minds.

DAILY QUERY 1

Read Genesis 12:1-5: The Lord said to Abram: Go out from your land, your relatives, and your father's house to the land that I will show you. I will make you into a great nation, I will bless you, I will make your name great, and you will be a blessing. I will bless those who bless you, I will curse anyone who treats you with contempt, and all the peoples on earth will be blessed through you. So Abram went, as the Lord had told him, and Lot went with him. Abram was seventy-five years old when he left Haran. He took his wife Sarai, his nephew Lot, all the possessions they had accumulated, and the people they had acquired in Haran, and they set out for the land of Canaan.

➤ What can I learn about God from these verses?

➤ What can I learn about Abram from these verses?

➤ Name one time you know God asked you to obey, and you did.

➤ Pray: Thank you, God, for helping me obey You …

DAILY QUERY 2

Read Genesis 15:5-6: He took him outside and said, "Look at the sky and count the stars, if you are able to count them." Then he said to him, "Your offspring will be that numerous." Abram believed the Lord, and he credited it to him as righteousness.

➤ How is this promise different than the one in Genesis 12 from yesterday?

➤ How do you think Abram felt when God promised him this?

➤ Name one way you think God is asking you to obey Him.

➤ Pray: Thank you, God, for your plan for me. Help me to follow it. These are places where I struggle to obey You sometimes …

DAILY QUERY 3

Read Genesis 15:18: On that day the Lord made a covenant with Abram, saying, "I give this land to your offspring."

➤ God made Abram a promise. God always keeps His promises. How good are you at keeping promises?

Not Dependable   Dependable

1   2   3   4   5   6   7   8   9   10

➤ Pray, thanking God that He keeps promises.

DAILY QUERY 4

Read Genesis 21:1-3: The Lord came to Sarah as he had said, and the Lord did for Sarah what he had promised. Sarah became pregnant and bore a son to Abraham in his old age, at the appointed time God had told him. Abraham named his son who was born to him—the one Sarah bore to him—Isaac.

➤ How do you think Abraham and Sarah felt when God promised them a baby?

➤ What is one way you know you can trust God?

➤ Pray: Thank you, God, for your plan for me. Help me to follow it. These are places where I struggle to obey You sometimes …

DAILY QUERY 5

Read Genesis 21:5-6: Abraham was a hundred years old when his son Isaac was born to him. Sarah said, "God has made me laugh, and everyone who hears will laugh with me."

➤ Look back at each day's query. Think about what you learned and whether it changed how you think about God and growing closer to Him. Answer each of the following questions:

➤ What truth did I discover this week?

➤ What did I learn about myself and Jesus?

➤ Is there anything I realized I need to confess to God and change?

The Quest & Fear

TRUSTING AND DEPENDING ON GOD

Pursue —
to find, to seek, to follow up

JESUS ACCOMPLISHED THE WORK OF SALVATION ON THE CROSS, BUT GOD PURSUES US TO HAVE A RESTORED RELATIONSHIP WITH HIM, JUST AS HE DID WITH ADAM AND EVE IN THE GARDEN.

JESUS CALMS THE STORM

Jesus spent all day teaching crowds of people near the Sea of Galilee. That evening, Jesus wanted to cross over to the other side of the sea. He said, "Let's cross over to the other side of the lake."

So Jesus and His disciples left the crowds. They got into a boat and began sailing. Some of the people from the crowds followed in their own boats. While Jesus and His disciples traveled, Jesus fell asleep on a cushion at the back of the boat.

All of a sudden, a storm came. The wind was strong, and the waves crashed into the boat. Water was coming into the boat, and the disciples were afraid! Many of the disciples were fishermen. They had survived storms on the sea before, but this storm was different. It was so strong. If the water kept coming in the boat, the boat would sink. Surely they would all drown!

The disciples looked to Jesus for help, but Jesus was still fast asleep at the back of the boat. He didn't seem to even notice the storm. Did Jesus care that they were about to sink into the sea?

The disciples woke up Jesus. "Lord, save us!" they said. "We are going to die!"

Jesus opened His eyes and saw that His friends were afraid. He got up and spoke to the wind. Then Jesus said to the sea, "Silence! Be still!"

At the sound of Jesus' voice, the wind stopped blowing and the waves stopped crashing. Everything was calm. The disciples were safe.

Jesus looked at His disciples and asked, "Why are you afraid? Do you still have no faith?" Did the disciples not trust Jesus to take care of them?

The disciples were amazed. "Who is this man?" they asked each other. "Even the wind and the waves obey Him!"

— based on Matthew 8:23-27; Mark 4:35-41; Luke 8:22-25

KEYBOARD CRAZINESS!

This keyboard is going crazy. When someone types the letters, different letters show up on the screen. The screen prints the letter that is one row down and slightly to the left. Can you figure out the words from the screen?

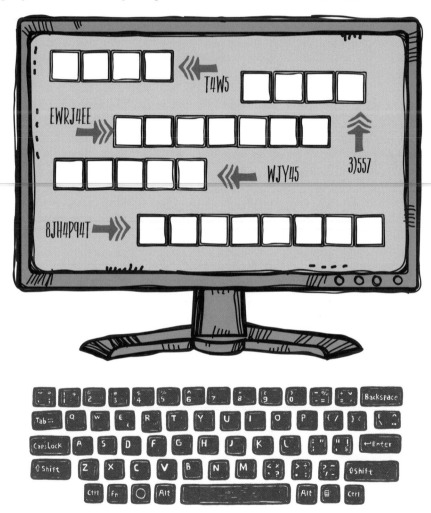

Can you think of other obstacles to write in code? Now try decoding some ways to overcome obstacles to growing closer to God!

54P7   0J   Y0R   H4   EW69ET94R   396U   3UW6   708   UWG4

Create some of your own codes:

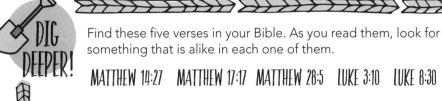

Find these five verses in your Bible. As you read them, look for something that is alike in each one of them.

MATTHEW 14:27   MATTHEW 17:17   MATTHEW 28:5   LUKE 3:10   LUKE 8:30

What did you find that was alike? Could it be an obstacle to growing closer to God? Now look up these two verses to find what can help you overcome the obstacle.

GENESIS 26:24   JOSHUA 1:9

Did you find it? To find out if you are right, unscramble these letters.

OG'DS   SENPRECE

TRUSTING GOD

This camper parking lot has hidden words in it. Can you find five or more words from this meeting's Bible story found in Luke 8:22-25? Circle those words. When you find those words, draw a triangle around them. See how many you can find!

MY DAILY QUERIES

Queries are just another name for questions. At the end of each week's study, you will have two pages to use privately as you talk to God, ask Him questions, and seek to grow closer to Him.

DAILY QUERY 1

Read Luke 8:22-24: One day he and his disciples got into a boat, and he told them, "Let's cross over to the other side of the lake." So they set out, and as they were sailing he fell asleep. Then a fierce windstorm came down on the lake; they were being swamped and were in danger. They came and woke him up, saying, "Master, Master, we're going to die!" Then he got up and rebuked the wind and the raging waves. So they ceased, and there was a calm.

➤ What is something you learned about the disciples in these verses?

_____

➤ List some times you are afraid below.
_____ _____ _____ _____

➤ Pray about your fear and thank God that He is powerful to help you.

DAILY QUERY 2

Read Luke 8:25: He said to them, "Where is your faith?" They were fearful and amazed, asking one another, "Who then is this? He commands even the winds and the waves, and they obey him!"

➤ What can I learn about Jesus from these verses?
➤ List some words that describe Jesus in this story.

_____ _____ _____ _____

➤ Praise God that He is powerful to help you in times of danger.

DAILY QUERY 3

Read Mark 4:35-41: On that day, when evening had come, he told them, "Let's cross over to the other side of the sea." So they left the crowd and took him along since he was in the boat. And other boats were with him. A great windstorm arose, and the waves were breaking over the boat, so that the boat was already being swamped. He was in the stern, sleeping on the cushion. So they woke him up and said to him, "Teacher! Don't you care that we're going to die?" He got up, rebuked the wind, and said to the sea, "Silence! Be still!" The wind ceased, and there was a great calm. Then he said to them, "Why are you afraid? Do you still have no faith?" And they were terrified and asked one another, "Who then is this? Even the wind and the sea obey him!"

➤ What can I learn about Jesus from these verses?

➤ What was Jesus doing while the disciples began to fear the storm?

➤ Why do you think Jesus had such peace?

➤ Describe one time God helped you have peace in a difficult situation?

➤ Pray, asking God to help you remember to turn to Him first when you need help.

DAILY QUERY 4

Read Matthew 8:23-27: As he got into the boat, his disciples followed him. Suddenly, a violent storm arose on the sea, so that the boat was being swamped by the waves—but Jesus kept sleeping. So the disciples came and woke him up, saying, "Lord, save us! We're going to die!" He said to them, "Why are you afraid, you of little faith?" Then he got up and rebuked the winds and the sea, and there was a great calm. The men were amazed and asked, "What kind of man is this? Even the winds and the sea obey him!"

➤ Why would Jesus let them sail into a storm like this?

➤ How did fear keep the disciples from growing closer to God at first?

➤ Jesus does not cause bad things to happen but sometimes allows them to help test us so that we will trust Him more. What is one time you needed help and prayed to God?

➤ Pray, thanking God for His help in times of trouble.

DAILY QUERY 5

➤ Look back at each day's query. Think about what you learned and whether it changed how you think about God and growing closer to Him. Answer each of the following questions:

➤ What truth did I discover this week?

➤ What did I learn about myself and Jesus?

➤ Is there anything I realized I need to confess to God and change?

The Quest
& Difficult Times

CLINGING CLOSE TO GOD

Explore —
to investigate, study, or analyze,
to become familiar with by testing

or experimenting

GOD WANTS US TO EXPLORE GOING
DEEPER WITH HIM BY TRUSTING HIM THROUGH
THE GOOD AND BAD THINGS IN LIFE. GOD
KEEPS HIS PROMISES TO US, AND WE CAN
TRUST HIM TO DO WHAT HE SAYS.

JOSEPH'S LIFE

Joseph was born to Jacob and Rachael and had 11 brothers. When Joseph was 17 years old, his job was to help his brothers care for the sheep. Jacob loved Joseph more than his other children. He gave Joseph a beautiful robe of many colors. The brothers were jealous. Joseph told his family about dreams he had where he was a ruler over them. That just made them more jealous.

One day, the brothers saw Joseph coming and decided to kill him. They threw him in a pit and considered what to do. Finally, they sold Joseph as a slave to a group on its way to Egypt. The brothers rubbed goat blood on Joseph's coat and used it to convince their father that Joseph was dead.

When Joseph got to Egypt, he was sold as a slave to Potiphar, the captain of the guard. God was with Joseph and made everything he did successful. Soon Joseph was in charge of everything Potiphar owned. However, Potiphar's wife told him a terrible lie about Joseph. Potiphar was so angry, he had Joseph thrown in jail.

God was with Joseph in the jail. He caused the jailer to like Joseph. Soon Joseph was in charge of all the prisoners in the jail. One day two men in the jail had dreams that Joseph explained for them. Later one of the men remembered that Joseph could tell about dreams. He told Pharaoh about Joseph and Joseph was called to Pharaoh's court.

With God's help, Joseph successfully told Pharaoh about his dream and the coming famine. Pharaoh put Joseph in charge of everything in Egypt so that his country could survive the famine that was to come. Pharaoh made Joseph second in command over all of Egypt. He gave Joseph a ring, a robe, and a gold chain—symbols of the power that he was handing over to Joseph.

The famine spread all the way back to Joseph's home in Canaan. His father Jacob sent ten of the brothers to Egypt to get food. They had no idea they would be asking Joseph for what they needed! Joseph recognized his brothers, but they didn't recognize him. Joseph tested them and found they had become trustworthy men. When he told them who he was, he invited them to bring the whole family to live in Egypt where he could be sure they had food.

The whole family moved to Egypt. Jacob and Joseph were so glad to see each other again and rejoiced that God provided for them. After many years, Jacob died. Joseph's brothers worried that Joseph would harm them in revenge for what they had done to him. Instead, Joseph said, "Don't be afraid. You planned evil for me, but God planned it for good. See the survival of so many people! Don't be afraid. I will take care of you."

—based on various passages in Genesis 37–50

HOW?

How can a person cling to God during hard times?
Look at this packing list for a hike. Can you find one answer to the question?

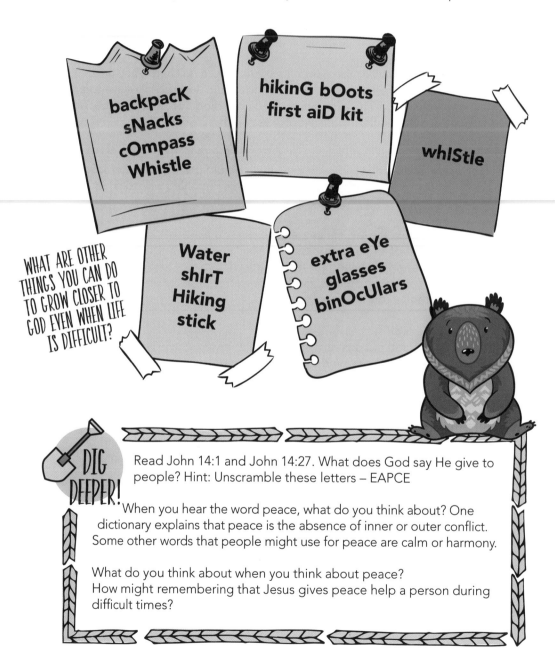

backpacK
sNacks
cOmpass
Whistle

hikinG bOots
first aiD kit

whIStle

WHAT ARE OTHER THINGS YOU CAN DO TO GROW CLOSER TO GOD EVEN WHEN LIFE IS DIFFICULT?

Water
shIrT
Hiking
stick

extra eYe
glasses
binOcUlars

DIG DEEPER!

Read John 14:1 and John 14:27. What does God say He give to people? Hint: Unscramble these letters – EAPCE

When you hear the word peace, what do you think about? One dictionary explains that peace is the absence of inner or outer conflict. Some other words that people might use for peace are calm or harmony.

What do you think about when you think about peace?
How might remembering that Jesus gives peace help a person during difficult times?

JOSEPH'S QUEST

Find your way through the woods! Start at the top of the path. Read the sentence near the top. Using the words below, fill in the blanks of the sentence. Decide whether the sentence is something good that happened to Joseph, something bad that happened, or both! Keep going all the way through the path.

WORDS: brothers, care, charge, famine, food, forgave, jail, pit, robe, slave, work

Joseph was now a _____, but God blessed his _____.

Joseph's dad gave him a _____, but his brothers put him in a _____.

Potiphar's wife lied about Joseph and he was put in _____.

Pharaoh told Joseph his dreams. Joseph told him a _____ was coming.

Joseph _____ his brothers.

Pharaoh put Joseph in _____ of all Egypt's _____.

Joseph's _____ came to get food in Egypt.

Joseph brought his brothers to Egypt where he could _____ for them.

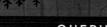

MY DAILY QUERIES

Each day has a Bible passage for you to read and think about. It may have questions to spark your thinking or explanations about the verses. Each day has space for you to journal your thoughts, feelings, and questions to God. It's true that God knows our thoughts whether we write them or not, but sometimes writing them helps us get things more firmly fixed in our hearts and minds. OK. Ready, set, query!

DAILY QUERY 1

Read Genesis 37:3-4. Now Israel loved Joseph more than his other sons because Joseph was a son born to him in his old age, and he made a robe of many colors for him. When his brothers saw that their father loved him more than all his brothers, they hated him and could not bring themselves to speak peaceably to him.

➤ What do you learn about Joseph's father and his brothers?
Joseph's father, Israel (Isaac): _____
Joseph's brothers: _____

➤ What might you have done as a brother in the same situation?

➤ Write down the name of someone to pray for in your family. Pray that God will help you live to honor Him in how you treat your family.
_____

DAILY QUERY 2

Read Genesis 37:5-7: Then Joseph had a dream. When he told it to his brothers, they hated him even more. He said to them, "Listen to this dream I had: There we were, binding sheaves of grain in the field. Suddenly my sheaf stood up, and your sheaves gathered around it and bowed down to my sheaf."

➤ What do you learn about Joseph from these verses?

➤ Why do you think he told his brothers his dream?

➤ Do you ever have times you get jealous of your siblings or friends?

➤ Pray that God will help you with feelings of jealousy or times you don't get along with friends.

DAILY QUERY 3

Read Genesis 37:23-24: When Joseph came to his brothers, they stripped off Joseph's robe, the robe of many colors that he had on. Then they took him and threw him into the pit. The pit was empty, without water.

➤ Why did Joseph's brothers do this terrible thing to Joseph?
_____

➤ How do you think Joseph felt? _____

➤ Do you believe God was with Joseph in the pit? _____

➤ Have you ever had a situation that seemed hopeless, but you saw later that God was still there taking care of you?

➤ Pray, thanking God for being with you even in the worst of times.

DAILY QUERY 4

Read Genesis 39:19-23. Now Joseph had been taken to Egypt. An Egyptian named Potiphar, an officer of Pharaoh and the captain of the guards, bought him from the Ishmaelites who had brought him there. The Lord was with Joseph, and he became a successful man, serving in the household of his Egyptian master.

➤ Was God with Joseph even after he was sold as a slave? _____

➤ Is God watching you even when no one else you know is around?

➤ What questions does this verse make you think about?

➤ Pray, thanking God for how He cares for you even when it feels like you are all alone.

DAILY QUERY 5

Read Genesis 50:20: You planned evil against me; God planned it for good to bring about the present result—the survival of many people.

➤ One day Joseph would meet his brothers again and tell them, "You planned evil against me; God planned it for good." Praise God that He brings about good things out of terrible situations!

➤ Look back at each day's query. Think about what you learned and whether it changed how you think about God and growing closer to Him. Answer each of the following questions:

➤ What truth did I discover this week?

➤ What did I learn about myself and Jesus?

The Quest & Others

GROWING CLOSER TO GOD
THROUGH SERVICE

Inquire —
to ask about, to search into,
to make investigation

GOD WANTS US TO ASK HIM QUESTIONS. IT SHOWS WE WANT TO KNOW AND UNDERSTAND HIM MORE AND ARE SEEKING TO FIND ANSWERS. GOD ASKS US QUESTIONS TO DRAW US CLOSER TO HIM.

BREAKFAST WITH JESUS

Jesus asked Peter, "Do you love Me more than these?"

Peter answered, "Yes Lord. You know I love You."

"Feed my lambs," Jesus said.

Again Jesus asked Peter, "Son of John, do you love Me?"

"You know I love You," Peter answered.

"Take care of My sheep," Jesus said.

"Simon, do you love Me?" Jesus asked.

Peter was hurt that Jesus asked him this question a third time. "You know everything, Lord," he said. "You know I love You."

"Feed my sheep. When you were young, you took care of yourself. When you are old, you will need help to take care of yourself."

Jesus wanted Peter to know how he would glorify God. Then Jesus said, "Follow Me."

When Peter looked around and saw John following them, he asked Jesus, "What about Him?"

Jesus said, "If I want him to live until I come back, what is that to you. YOU follow Me."

Jesus didn't say that John would live that long. He just meant that it was not Peter's business.

John wrote that Jesus did so many things that if they were written down, the world could not hold them all!

—based on John 21:15-25

RING OF FIRE

Play this game with a friend. Use dimes for gamepieces. Mark one side of a button with an X. Toss the button. If the X lands on top, hop into the first space. If the X lands on bottom, hop into the second log. Read the question where you land. After you answer the question, mark out the space with a big X. Now let your friend toss the button. X on top means move one space; X on bottom means to move two spaces. BUT only count the spaces that are not marked out. Play until all the spaces are marked out.

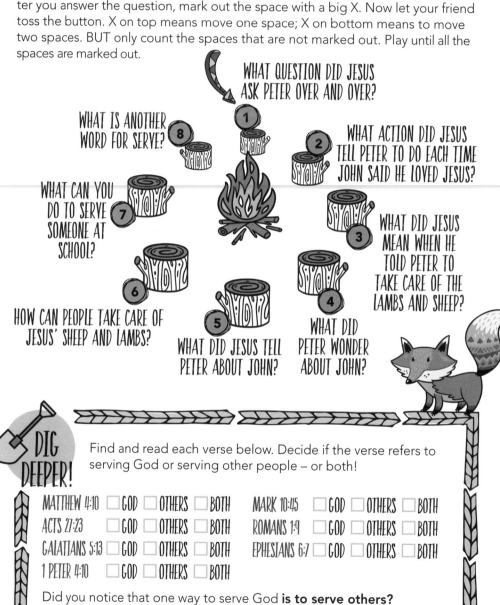

1 WHAT QUESTION DID JESUS ASK PETER OVER AND OVER?

2 WHAT ACTION DID JESUS TELL PETER TO DO EACH TIME JOHN SAID HE LOVED JESUS?

8 WHAT IS ANOTHER WORD FOR SERVE?

7 WHAT CAN YOU DO TO SERVE SOMEONE AT SCHOOL?

3 WHAT DID JESUS MEAN WHEN HE TOLD PETER TO TAKE CARE OF THE LAMBS AND SHEEP?

6 HOW CAN PEOPLE TAKE CARE OF JESUS' SHEEP AND LAMBS?

5 WHAT DID JESUS TELL PETER ABOUT JOHN?

4 WHAT DID PETER WONDER ABOUT JOHN?

DIG DEEPER!

Find and read each verse below. Decide if the verse refers to serving God or serving other people – or both!

	GOD	OTHERS	BOTH		GOD	OTHERS	BOTH
MATTHEW 4:10	☐	☐	☐	MARK 10:45	☐	☐	☐
ACTS 27:23	☐	☐	☐	ROMANS 1:9	☐	☐	☐
GALATIANS 5:13	☐	☐	☐	EPHESIANS 6:7	☐	☐	☐
1 PETER 4:10	☐	☐	☐				

Did you notice that one way to serve God **is to serve others?**

YOUR SERVE

In each group, choose whether the **TENT** or the **MOUNTAIN** describes how a servant of God can help others. Circle the one you've chosen.

E WITH LOVE	**S** ANGRILY
U SLOWLY	**V** ENCOURAGING
R HAPPILY	**S** UNCONCERNED
E HUMBLY	**E** UPSET
J RELUCTANTLY	**S** CARING

Now, print the letter inside each circled tent or mountain to find another word for helping others. (Oh, yes, start from the bottom and go up!)

Who is our best example of doing this? Print the letters beside the uncircled boots, from bottom to top.

MY DAILY QUERIES

Queries are just another name for questions. It's true that God knows our thoughts whether we write them or not, but sometimes writing them helps us get things more firmly fixed in our hearts and minds. OK. Ready, set, query!

DAILY QUERY 1

Read John 21:3-6: "I'm going fishing," Simon Peter said to them.
"We're coming with you," they told him. They went out and got into the boat, but that night they caught nothing. When daybreak came, Jesus stood on the shore, but the disciples did not know it was Jesus.
"Friends," Jesus called to them, "you don't have any fish, do you?"
"No," they answered. "Cast the net on the right side of the boat," he told them, "and you'll find some." So they did, and they were unable to haul it in because of the large number of fish.

➤ Why did Jesus help them catch fish?

➤ Why do you think the disciples didn't realize Jesus was standing on the shore?

➤ What might you have done in the same situation?

➤ Pray, asking God to make it clear to you when He is speaking to you.

DAILY QUERY 2

Read John 21:7-11: The disciple, the one Jesus loved, said to Peter, "It is the Lord!" When Simon Peter heard that it was the Lord, he tied his outer clothing around him (for he had taken it off) and plunged into the sea. Since they were not far from land (about a hundred yards away), the other disciples came in the boat, dragging the net full of fish. When they got out on land, they saw a charcoal fire there, with fish lying on it, and bread. "Bring some of the fish you've just caught," Jesus told them. So Simon Peter climbed up and hauled the net ashore, full of large fish—153 of them. Even though there were so many, the net was not torn.

➤ What do you notice about what Jesus says to the disciples?

➤ How might Peter and John have felt?

➤ Why did Peter jump out of the boat? Would you have done the same?

➤ Pray, asking God to help you be bold like Peter and confident like John.

DAILY QUERY 3

Read John 21:12-14: "Come and have breakfast," Jesus told them. None of the disciples dared ask him, "Who are you?" because they knew it was the Lord. Jesus came, took the bread, and gave it to them. He did the same with the fish. This was now the third time Jesus appeared to the disciples after he was raised from the dead.

➤ What do you learn about the disciples from this passage?

➤ Why do you think that Jesus appeared to the disciples multiple times?

➤ Do you think that Jesus wants people to know Him so much that He gives them many chances to get to know Him?

➤ Pray, thanking God for seeking after you.

DAILY QUERY 4

Read John 21:15-17: When they had eaten breakfast, Jesus asked Simon Peter, "Simon, son of John, do you love me more than these?"

"Yes, Lord," he said to him, "you know that I love you."

"Feed my lambs," he told him. A second time he asked him, "Simon, son of John, do you love me?"

"Yes, Lord," he said to him, "you know that I love you."

"Shepherd my sheep," he told him. He asked him the third time, "Simon, son of John, do you love me?"

Peter was grieved that he asked him the third time, "Do you love me?" He said, "Lord, you know everything; you know that I love you."

"Feed my sheep," Jesus said.

➤ What do you learn about Jesus and Peter from these verses?

➤ Why do you think Jesus asked Peter the same question three times?

➤ How was Peter to show his love for Jesus?

➤ What might you do if Jesus asked you to serve Him?

➤ Pray, asking God to show you who He wants you to serve.

DAILY QUERY 5

Read John 21:18-19: "Truly I tell you, when you were younger, you would tie your belt and walk wherever you wanted. But when you grow old, you will stretch out your hands and someone else will tie you and carry you where you don't want to go." He said this to indicate by what kind of death Peter would glorify God. After saying this, he told him, "Follow me."

Look back at each day's query. Answer each of the following questions:
➤ What truth did I discover this week?

➤ What did I learn about myself and Jesus?

➤ Is there anything I realized I need to confess to God and change?

The Quest & Promise

GOD WILL GO WITH US TO THE END

Examine —

to inspect closely, to test the condition of,

to inquire into carefully

LIFE HAS A WAY OF TESTING US. GOD WANTS US TO EXAMINE EVERY CIRCUMSTANCE IN LIFE, SEE HIS PLAN FOR US, AND SEEK HOW HE WANTS US TO OBEY HIM.

DAVID WAS ANOINTED AND FOUGHT GOLIATH

Saul was not going to be king of Israel anymore. He had disobeyed God. Israel needed a new king, a better king. God told Samuel to visit a man in Bethlehem named Jesse. Jesse had eight sons, and one of them would be Israel's king. Samuel did what God told him to do. He went to Bethlehem to meet with Jesse and his sons. Jesse's oldest son, Eliab, was tall and handsome.

"This must be the one God chose to be king," Samuel thought. "Samuel, he's not the one," God said. "Do not pay attention to what he looks like. You look at what you can see on the outside, but I see the heart." One by one, Jesse's sons approached Samuel, but God had not chosen any of them. "Do you have any more sons?" Samuel asked. "Yes," Jesse said. "My youngest son, David, is in the field taking care of the sheep." Jesse sent for David. When David arrived, God told Samuel, "He's the one!"

Samuel poured oil on David's head and the Spirit of the Lord was with David. Then Samuel went back home. The Spirit of the Lord was not with Saul anymore. In fact, Saul was bothered by an evil spirit. Saul's servants suggested Saul find someone who could play the harp. Hearing beautiful music might make Saul feel better when the evil spirit bothered him. One of Saul's officials knew just the person to play the harp—David, son of Jesse. David came to Saul and whenever Saul felt troubled, David played his harp and Saul felt better.

At this time, Israel's enemies, the Philistines, got ready for war. They were going to attack a town in Judah. King Saul got his army ready to fight. The Israelites camped on one hill while the Philistines camped on another. There was a valley between them. The Philistines had a great warrior named Goliath. At 9 feet 9 inches tall, Goliath was their hero. Goliath shouted at the Israelites, "Why are you lined up, ready for battle? Send me your best man, and we'll fight one-on-one." But none of the Israelites wanted to fight Goliath. They were afraid of him.

Jesse's three oldest sons were part of the Israelite army camped on a hill. Jesse sent David to check on his brothers and to give them something to eat. David saw Goliath and watched the Israelites run away in fear. David heard that Saul had offered a great reward to the man who killed Goliath, and David volunteered to fight. "You don't stand a chance against Goliath," Saul argued. "I have killed wild animals," David explained. "God will keep me safe." Saul allowed David to fight Goliath. He offered his armor to David, but David could hardly move. He took off the armor and chose five smooth stones from a nearby stream. David was armed only with the stones and a slingshot. Goliath saw David and made fun of him because he was just a boy. "You come to fight with a spear and sword," David replied, "but I come to fight in the name of God! You have insulted Him, and God always wins His battles!" David ran toward Goliath. He slung a rock at Goliath, and the rock hit Goliath in the forehead. Goliath fell facedown, and David killed him without even having a sword.

-based on 1 Samuel 16—17

BLOCK LETTERS

Fill in the answers to the clues. Then fill in the blanks in the sentence, using the letters in the clues. Find the answer to the question: What do I need for my quest?

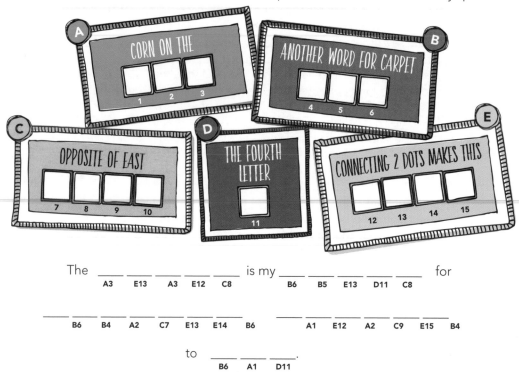

A CORN ON THE
⬚ ⬚ ⬚
1 2 3

B ANOTHER WORD FOR CARPET
⬚ ⬚ ⬚
4 5 6

C OPPOSITE OF EAST
⬚ ⬚ ⬚ ⬚
7 8 9 10

D THE FOURTH LETTER
⬚
11

E CONNECTING 2 DOTS MAKES THIS
⬚ ⬚ ⬚ ⬚
12 13 14 15

The ___ ___ ___ ___ ___ is my ___ ___ ___ ___ ___ for
   A3 E13 A3 E12 C8   B6 B5 E13 D11 C8

___ ___ ___ ___ ___ ___ ___   ___ ___ ___ ___ ___ ___
B6 B4 A2 C7 E13 E14 B6   A1 E12 A2 C9 E15 B4

to ___ ___ ___.
   B6 A1 D11

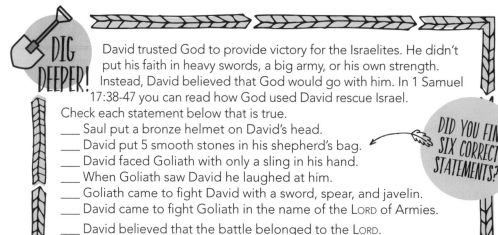

DIG DEEPER!

David trusted God to provide victory for the Israelites. He didn't put his faith in heavy swords, a big army, or his own strength. Instead, David believed that God would go with him. In 1 Samuel 17:38-47 you can read how God used David rescue Israel.

Check each statement below that is true.

___ Saul put a bronze helmet on David's head.
___ David put 5 smooth stones in his shepherd's bag.
___ David faced Goliath with only a sling in his hand.
___ When Goliath saw David he laughed at him.
___ Goliath came to fight David with a sword, spear, and javelin.
___ David came to fight Goliath in the name of the LORD of Armies.
___ David believed that the battle belonged to the LORD.

DID YOU FIND SIX CORRECT STATEMENTS?

MAKE A MATCH

Your Bible is helpful in knowing what to do in many situations. These owls don't say "Hoo Hoo?" They say "What? What?" Read the questions and draw line to the owl that could help you. Some owls might match to more than one question!

MY DAILY QUERIES

Although these are the last pages in your book, you can continue your queries with God. Grab a notebook, a pen or pencil, and your Bible. Keep them where you will be reminded to use them each day. Choose a book of the Bible, such as Mark, and read a few verses in that book each day. Record what you learn, how you feel, what God is teaching you, and anything you want to include.

DAILY QUERY 1

Read Psalm 119:97-100: How I love your instruction! It is my meditation all day long. Your commands make me wiser than my enemies, for they are always with me. I have more insight than all my teachers because your decrees are my meditation. I understand more than the elders because I obey your precepts.

➤ What do you learn about God's Word?

➤ How do these Bible verses make you feel?

➤ In what ways might you be wise and understanding if you study and obey God's Word?

➤ Pray, asking God to show you the way He wants you to live.

DAILY QUERY 2

Read Psalm 119:111-112: I have your decrees as a heritage forever; indeed, they are the joy of my heart. I am resolved to obey your statutes to the very end.

➤ How long will God's Word lead you?

➤ What about the Bible makes you feel joy?

➤ What does God want you to learn from these verses?

➤ Pray, asking God to help you study the Bible regularly.

DAILY QUERY 3

Read Psalm 119:129-132: Your decrees are wondrous; therefore I obey them. The revelation of your words brings light and gives understanding to the inexperienced. I open my mouth and pant because I long for your commands. Turn to me and be gracious to me, as is your practice toward those who love your name.

➤ What are two of God's commands, decrees, or statutes you find wonderful?

➤ Why might King David have thought God's laws are wonderful?

➤ What does God want you to learn from these verses?

➤ Pray, thanking God for teaching you through the Bible.

DAILY QUERY 4

Read Psalm 119:133-136: Make my steps steady through your promise; don't let any sin dominate me. Redeem me from human oppression, and I will keep your precepts. Make your face shine on your servant, and teach me your statutes. My eyes pour out streams of tears because people do not follow your instruction.

➤ How might sin rule a person's life?

➤ How can the Bible help a person stay away from sin ruling his life?

➤ What examples can you recall of people following God's instructions and help them stop making bad choices?

➤ Pray, asking God for forgiveness of your sins.

DAILY QUERY 5

Read Psalm 119:171-173: My lips pour out praise, for you teach me your statutes. My tongue sings about your promise, for all your commands are righteous. May your hand be ready to help me, for I have chosen your precepts.

➤ What do you want to praise God for doing or being?

➤ What promises has God made? Is He keeping those promises?

➤ Write down all the words in these verses that mean God's Word. How do you feel about their being so many?

Look back at each day's query. Answer each of the following questions:

➤ What truth did I discover this week?

➤ What did I learn about myself and Jesus?

➤ Is there anything I realized I need to confess to God and change?

THE QUEST: GROWING CLOSER TO GOD IS OUR QUEST

This week we are focusing on people as God's prized creation, made in His image. Despite the rebellion of sin, because of God's great love for us, He made a plan to rescue us by sending His Son, Jesus.

KEY VERSE: "Ask, and it will be given to you. Seek, and you will find. Knock, and the door will be opened to you." Matthew 7:7

BIBLE STORY PASSAGE:
Genesis 1—3

TEACHING POINTS

➤ Talk about a quest. The Quest for Kids is about the adventure (quest) of knowing more about God.

➤ Review Genesis 1—3. Emphasize people are God's prized creation. He created us in His image, declared us very good, and desires to have a lasting relationship with us. Despite the rebellion of sin, because of God's great love for us, He made a plan to rescue us by sending His Son, Jesus. God desires to bring us back into a restored relationship with Him, so that we know God, grow closer to Him, and walk with Him day by day.

➤ Talk about how asking questions is one important way we learn about the world around us. God wants us to ask Him questions. It shows we want to know and understand Him more.

BIBLE STORY

Read today's Bible story about Adam and Eve in Genesis 1—3. Ask the following review questions:
Q1: How did God create everything?
A1: He spoke everything into existence. (Genesis 1.)

Q2: How did God describe everything He created?
A2: God said, "It is good." (Genesis 1.)
Q3: How are man and woman special?
A3: Man and woman are created in the image of God. (Genesis 1:27)
Q4: How did the serpent trick Eve?
A4: Told her the fruit would make her like God (Genesis 3:3)
Q6: After Adam and Eve ate, what did they do when they heard God?
A6: They hid in the garden. (Genesis 3:8)
Q7: What question did God ask Adam after Adam hid?
A7: Where are you? (Genesis 3:9)
Q8: What hope did God give Adam and Eve?
A8: God promised that He would send a Savior, and God clothed them. (Genesis 3:15,21)

GO DEEPER

Q9: What words can you use to describe God?
A9: Loving, forgiving, Creator, etc.

PRAY AND JOURNAL

➤ Complete pages 10-11 together.

ACTIVITY

➤ Use sheets of paper to make a path. Each time your child tells a fact about today's Bible story, she advances two spaces. Let your child create questions for you to answer about the Bible story.

THE QUEST AND FAITH: FOLLOWING GOD'S PLAN

This week we are focusing on following God's leading, whether anything is too hard for God, and the ultimate promise that God will right every wrong at some time. The Gospel will be presented to kids after discussing Abraham's faith.

KEY VERSE: "For everyone who asks receives, and the one who seeks finds, and to the one who knocks, the door will be opened." Matthew 7:8

BIBLE STORY PASSAGE:
Genesis 12:1-5 and 15:1-6

TEACHING POINTS
➤ Growing closer to God is a quest that lasts a lifetime.

➤ God planned each person's journey before the person was ever born.

➤ God sent His Son Jesus to be the Savior and bring people back to Himself.

➤ Today we will learn how Abraham spent his life growing closer to God.

BIBLE STORY
Abraham's story takes up several chapters in Genesis. Read together Genesis 12:1-5 and 15:1-6 to find ways Abraham obeyed God. Ask the following review questions:
Q1: Where did God tell Abram to go?
A1: To a land He would show Abram (Gen.12:1)
Q2: Who did Abram take with him?
A2: Sarai, Lot, and his servants (Gen. 12:5)
Q3: How many children did God promise to Abram?
A2: More than the stars in the sky (Gen. 15:3)
Q4: How did Abram respond to God's promise?

A4: He believed what God said (Gen. 15:6)

GO DEEPER
Q5: What do you think God wants us to learn from the story of Abram?
A5: God is pleased when people obey Him. God can do anything.
Q6: What kinds of plans might God have for your life?

PRAY AND JOURNAL
➤ Complete pages 16-17 together as you pray and write about what God is teaching you.

ACTIVITY
Make a GCTGTM (Growing Closer to God Text Message) Shelf Minder:
➤ Form a body shape from chenille stems.

➤ Abbreviate a message about growing closer to God to be like a text message (such as LOL for laughing out loud). Write it on a small rectangle of paper.

➤ Tape the message to one hand of the body shape.

➤ Place the shelf minder on a book shelf, a table, or other flat surface in your home.

THE QUEST AND FEAR: TRUSTING AND DEPENDING ON GOD

This week focuses on trusting and depending on God during times of fear. Jesus has power over anything we might fear and over all creation. Kids can learn that Jesus is stronger than anything that might be standing in their way of trusting God.

KEY VERSE: "Who among you, if his son asks him for bread, will give him a stone?" Matthew 7:9

BIBLE STORY PASSAGE:
Matthew 8:23-27

TEACHING POINTS
➤ Read Matthew 8:26 together to introduce the question Jesus asked the disciples.

➤ Talk together about times you are afraid and how you can trust God to care for you.

➤ Continue on the quest to learn more about trusting and depending on God.

BIBLE STORY
Read about the disciples on the lake in Matthew 8:23-27. Ask the following review questions:
Q1: What was happening to the boat?
A1: It was sinking (Matthew 8:24)
Q1: What was Jesus doing during the storm?
A2: Sleeping! (Matthew 8:24)
Q3: What did Jesus do to the storm?
A3: Made it stop (Matthew 8:26)
Q4: How did the disciples feel?
A4: Amazed (Matthew 8:27)

GO DEEPER
Q5: What do you think God wants us to learn from the story of the disciples and the storm?
A5: Jesus is in control of everything and we have no need to fear.
Q6: Why might God not always take what we fear away?
A6: To help us learn to trust Him as we go through the fear and to remember His presence at all times.

PRAY AND JOURNAL
➤ Complete pages 22-23 together as you pray and write about what God is teaching you.

ACTIVITY
Make truth spinners:
➤ Guide your child to write on the shiny side of a used CD (with a permanent marker) two or three things he might do to increase his dependence on God.

➤ Place the CD on top of a marble so that the marble pushes up slightly through the hole in the CD. Twist the marble and watch the CD spin.

➤ Time how long the CD will spin. Try to make it spin longer.

➤ Remark that the spinner is fun but it is also a reminder that you and your child are on a lifetime quest with God, the One who is in control of everything.

THE QUEST AND DIFFICULT TIMES: CLINGING CLOSE TO GOD

This week we are focusing on what difficult times are, how God comforts people during those times, and His promise to ultimately take care of things. Kids will learn who they can go to for help.

KEY VERSE: "Or if he asks for a fish, will give him a snake?" Matthew 7:10

BIBLE STORY PASSAGE:
Various passages from Genesis 37—50

TEACHING POINTS
➤ Today we will learn how to grow closer to God even during difficult situations.

➤ Ask your child if he can think of a difficult situation in his life. Pray with him and ask God to take care of him and lead him through that difficult time.

BIBLE STORY
Read Genesis 37:12-36 about Joseph being sold into slavery.
Ask the following review questions:
Q1: Where did the brothers put Joseph?
A1: In a pit in the wilderness (Genesis 37:21)
Q2: What was Joseph wearing when his brothers trapped him?
A2: A colorful robe (Genesis 37:23)
Q3: What did Joseph's brothers do to him when they heard the caravan coming?
A3: Sold him as a slave (Genesis 37:28)

GO DEEPER
Q4: What was difficult for Joseph in this story?
A4: His brothers hated him and he was taken to a foreign country as a slave.
Q5: What do you think God wants us to learn from the Bible story?
A5: God will always be with us during hard times and will comfort us.

PRAY AND JOURNAL
➤ Complete pages 28-29 together as you pray and write about what God is teaching you.

ACTIVITY
Make "My Quest Paper Gliders"
➤ On a large paper strip, print two ways to grow closer to God. On a shorter strip, print *My Quest: Growing Closer to God.*

➤ *Slide one paper clip into an end of a straw with the narrower part of the clip inside the straw. Do the same on the other end.

➤ Roll both paper strips into circles and slide them into different clips on the straw with the circles lined up one behind the other.

➤ Toss the glider and try to say the words of Matthew 7:10 before it lands.

THE QUEST AND OTHERS: GROWING CLOSER TO GOD THROUGH SERVICE

This week focuses on how Jesus is faithful to forgive and redeem us, calling us to follow Him. As we follow Him, we are called to serve Him by serving others.

KEY VERSE: "If you then, who are evil, know how to give good gifts to your children, how much more will your Father in heaven give good things to those who ask him." Matthew 7:11

BIBLE STORY PASSAGE:
John 21:15-25

TEACHING POINTS
➤ Together read Matthew 7:11 to introduce how much more God cares for people than anyone else does.

➤ Today we will learn how to grow closer to God by serving Him and others.

BIBLE STORY
Read today's Bible story about Jesus and Peter in John 21:15—25.
Ask the following review questions:
Q1: How many times did Jesus ask if Peter loved Him?
A1: 3 (John 21:15, 16, 19)
Q2: What did Jesus tell Peter three times to do?
A2: Take care of His sheep (John 21:15, 16, 17)
Q3: Who was Peter to follow?
A3: Jesus (John 21:19)

GO DEEPER
Q4: What do you think God wants us to learn from the Bible story?
A4: Even when we sin, Jesus is faithful to forgive us and call us to serve Him.
Q5: How can people serve God?
A5: By obeying Him and caring for others

PRAY AND JOURNAL
➤ Complete pages 34-35 as you pray and write about what God is teaching you.

ACTIVITY
Perform an act of service by choosing one of these activities or another of your choice.
➤ Prepare and send a care package to a soldier.

➤ Work together at a shelter to sort clothing, serve a meal, or distribute groceries.

➤ Take cold bottled water to police departments, fire stations, or first responders.

➤ Gather gently used toys and deliver them to a family shelter.

THE QUEST AND PROMISE: GOD WILL GO WITH US TO THE END

This week focuses the fact that this journey lasts a lifetime. One major way people can grow closer to God all during their lives is to study God's Word because it has wisdom for them no matter their ages or circumstances. King David recognized the importance of God's Word and worked to do all he knew to do.

KEY VERSE: Review Matthew 7:7-11

BIBLE STORY PASSAGE:
1 Samuel 16—17

TEACHING POINTS
➤ Together read Psalm 119:105 to introduce the importance of God's Word to people.

➤ Ask, "Why do you think remembering Bible verses and stories is important?"

➤ Share favorite Bible verses with each other.

➤ Today we will learn how the Bible helps us grow closer to God for our entire lives.

BIBLE STORY
Read today's Bible story from this activity book or 1 Samuel 16—17. Ask the following review questions:
Q1: Who had God chosen to be the next king of Israel?
A1: David (1 Samuel 16:12)
Q2: What instrument did David play and compose songs to God using?
A2: A harp or lyre (1 Samuel 16:18)
Q3: How did God show He was with David?
A3: The Spirit of the Lord was on David. (1 Samuel 16:13)
Q4: What did David do in today's Bible story that showed He was willing to trust God?
A4: David fought Goliath. (1 Samuel 17)

GO DEEPER
Discussion Questions
Q4: What do you think God wants us to learn from the Bible story?
A4: God gives us direction for what to do and how to grow closer to Him.
Q5: How long does a person's quest for God continue?
Q5: For a lifetime!

PRAY AND JOURNAL
➤ Complete pages 42-43 together as you pray and write about what God is teaching you.

ACTIVITY
Create a Bible memory plan:
➤ Together print the words of these verses (or others you choose) on different index cards: 1 Corinthians 16:8; Psalm 13:10; Psalm 119:105; Ephesians 6:14; Ephesians 6:15; Ephesians 6:16; Ephesians 6:17; Ephesians 6:18; 2 Timothy 3:16; James 1:22.

➤ Cut light-weight cardboard into an easel shape. Stack the index cards and display them on the stand.

➤ Memorize the verse on the first card. Place it at the back of the stack. Choose another card the next day.

➤ Review the cards often.

Certificate of Completion

This certificate is awarded to

_____

on _____

(date)

For completing

THE QUEST FOR KIDS: AN EXPEDITION TOWARD A DEEPER RELATIONSHIP WITH GOD

_____

(PARENT OR LEADER'S SIGNATURE)